Unbreakable: A Survivor's Testimony

A Powerful Collection of Stories That Journey From TRAUMA TO TRIUMP

by

T. S. Edwards

That Journey From TRAUMA TO TRIUMP" at
info@terrordomeent.com

ISBN: 978-1-7356974-7-5 (Paperback)

ISBN: 978-1-7356974-8-2 (E-book)

www.TSEdwardsAuthor.com

Author's Note

It is with the deepest gratitude and appreciation that I extend my heartfelt thanks to all my old and new friends who have courageously shared their most intimate and heartfelt experiences. Your willingness to be vulnerable and open has been truly humbling, and I am honored to have the privilege of sharing your stories.

To my dear readers, please understand that revealing one's deepest pain is no easy feat. I encourage you to approach these stories with the utmost care, empathy, and non-judgment. These authors have entrusted me with their most cherished memories, and it is my sincere hope that you will receive them with the same reverence and respect.

I also extend an open invitation to all of you to consider sharing your own stories. The act of storytelling can be a powerful tool for healing, self-discovery, and connection. By sharing our experiences, we can find solace in the knowledge that we are not alone in our struggles and triumphs.

Once again, I express my heartfelt gratitude to the authors who have entrusted me with their narratives. Your courage and resilience are inspiring, and I pray your stories have the power to touch and transform the lives of those who read them. Thank you for your trust, your vulnerability, and your willingness to share your journeys with the world.

Social Media:

Instagram: @tsedwards_author

Website:

www.TSEdwardsAuthor.com

www.TerrorDomeEntertainment.com

Other Books Available on Amazon

- Articles of Life: A Collection of Short Memoir Essays of Managing Life

- The Adventures of Hildie and Carlos (Revised and Updated). We Are Going to Paris!

- The Adventures of Hildie and Carlos (Bilingual English/Mandarin Chinese Edition). We Are Going to Paris!

- The Adventures of Hildie and Carlos. We Are Going to Guam!

DEDICATION

To my kind and supportive husband, Kyon, who has accepted me with all my emotional scars and continues to love me despite them. You are a true blessing in my life.

To my daughter Thalea, and my beautiful granddaughter Hildie, you are the air I breathe and the reason I live. Your unwavering love and support keep me grounded and motivated.

To my brothers from another mother, Derrick, James, and Maurice, you have been my ride-or-die through it all. Your presence in my life is truly invaluable.

To all my contributing authors, close friends, and the Terror Dome Family, you all have touched my heart. Your friendships and support mean the world to me.

To the rest of my family, friends, and even those who doubted me, plotted against me, and were once my ex's, thank you for being a part of my life. No matter how great or small your contribution, it has shaped me into the person I am today.

And most importantly, to God, for continuing to be my ***Footprints in the Sand***, guiding me through life's challenges and always being there to carry me when I can no longer walk on my own.

I am grateful beyond measure for the love and support of all the incredible people in my life. You have all played a significant role in my journey, and I am honored to have you by my side.

Table Of Contents

AUTHOR'S NOTE 4

DEDICATION 7

INTRODUCTION 11

BREAKING THE SILENCE 14

THE DAY I STOPPED BEING A VICTIM BY T. S. EDWARDS 18

FROM HARDSHIP TO HOPE BY KYON EDWARDS 32

A GIRLHOOD PROMISE BY YANIQUE MCKOY 40

THE TRIUMPH OF SAVING MY MARRIAGE: A JOURNEY OF FAITH, HEALING, AND RESTORATION BY ANONYMOUS 1 56

THROUGH ZAY ZAY'S EYES: A STORY OF LOVE, LOSS, AND RESILIENCE BY P.P 63

BROTHERHOOD AND BETRAYAL BY ANONYMOUS 2 71

THE SMILE IS THE SCAR BY DETHRA U. GILES 78

BEYOND SURVIVAL: THRIVING AFTER A BRAIN TUMOR BY D. SMITH 88

FROM PAIN TO PURPOSE BY WYTISHIA BLY 95

MOMENT OF STILLNESS BY MAXINE WILLIAMS WRIGHT.. 99

FAITH OVER FEAR BY TEADRAMA 112

A JOURNEY FROM DARKNESS TO LIGHT BY ANONYMOUS 3 117

A JOURNEY OF SURVIVAL AND PURPOSE BY DANA "MZDANAK" JONES......................... 121

ABOUT T. S. EDWARDS AKA MIZZ ENTERTAINMENT....................................... 124

Introduction

My Prayer

God, guide me through this book, in the hope that my trauma can be a light for someone else lost in the darkness of their own battles. My life has been filled with many fights, where I was knocked down so hard I couldn't even stand, let alone walk.

But through it all, YOU carried me! YOU held me up! And YOU made sure I survived and THRIVED.

Let this book be a lifeline to others who feel like they are drowning. Just as You have carried me so many times, I pray that You carry them until they, too, can stand and walk on their own.

To My Readers

This book is a heartfelt celebration of resilience and the strength within each of us. It's a powerful collection of stories from diverse authors, including my own, that shines a light on incredible journeys of people who have faced extraordinary challenges, endured profound hardships, and found ways to transform pain into purpose.

These are not just tales of survival; they are deeply inspiring accounts of courage, personal growth, and an unwavering commitment to hope. Within these pages, you'll meet individuals who have risen from life's darkest moments with renewed strength, wisdom, and clarity. You'll witness the determination it takes to find light even in the shadows, to heal and rebuild, and to turn struggle into meaning.

This collection resonates with universal truths and emotions, offering something for everyone. Whether you're in the midst of your own challenges or simply seeking inspiration, these stories are a reminder that, no matter how difficult the journey, we are never truly alone. Let the voices within these pages bring you comfort and encouragement, renewing your belief in the power of resilience and the guiding presence of God or a higher power. May these stories remind you that hope is always within reach, even in the most challenging times.

T. S. Edwards

Breaking the Silence

Surviving, healing, and finding your way back when life has knocked you down so hard you thought you'd never get up again—it's hard. I understand your pain and your struggle. Trauma isn't just something that happens to you; it's something that lives inside you, whispering lies, making you feel small and broken. But guess what? You are so much more than what happened to you.

Every single one of us has a story. Some days, I felt like I was drowning; other days, I saw a glimmer of hope. And that's okay. Healing isn't about being perfect—it's about being honest with yourself, about being 100% true to who you are.

Trauma loves silence. It thrives in those quiet spaces where you're afraid to speak, afraid to feel. But breaking that silence is like breaking free. When you start to talk about your experiences, when you allow yourself to feel the emotions you've been pushing down, that's when real healing begins.

There's an old cliché about forgiveness: *"Forgiveness isn't for them; it's for you."* People say this all the time, and as overused as it is... it's true. Forgiveness isn't about letting the person who hurt you off the hook. It's about letting yourself off the hook. It's about freeing yourself from the weight of anger, shame, and regret. It's about forgiving yourself—for surviving, for the ways you protected yourself, for the times you couldn't.

And those scars you're carrying? They're not marks of weakness; they're badges of honor. Every crack tells a story of survival and resilience. You didn't just survive—you're learning to thrive.

I collected these stories to remind you that you are not alone. These are my stories and the stories of my friends, shared with the hope that they will help each and every one of you. Healing can come in many forms—therapy, support groups, or even just talking to a friend who truly understands. Connection is key. Connection is healing. Your pain doesn't define you, but how you move through it does.

Writing helped me. Maybe it'll help you too. Put pen to paper. Share your story, even if it's just for yourself. Writing is a way to recognize that your experiences have given you a strength most people will never understand. When you start to make sense of your journey, you transform from a survivor into something greater. You transform into a *thriver*.

To anyone reading this who is in the middle of their healing journey—whether you're just starting, or you've been working at it for years—I see you. Your story matters. Your voice deserves to be heard. You are UNBREAKABLE!

And if you want to share your story and/or be on the podcast, send an email, "Attention: I Want To Share My Story" to *info@terrordomeent.com*.

The Day I Stopped Being A Victim by T. S. Edwards

The summer of '91 was a turning point in my life. I had gone to the movies with a "so-called" girlfriend, expecting a fun and carefree outing. Little did I know that day would mark the end of my time as a victim.

Before I get into that day, I need to do a brief recap of what led up to this day.

So, let's rewind...

As I detail in my book, "Articles of Life: A Collection of Short Memoir Essays of Managing Life," my childhood was marred by abuse—from being molested by family members to being raped by my mother's boyfriend before the age of 10. Let's just say my sense of self-worth was in the trash. These traumatic experiences had a devastating impact on my sense of self-worth and my perception of relationships, leading me down a path of self-destruction. My thoughts around sex were: Anyone can do anything to me, and the only thing I can do is just take it. So, by the age of 13, I was having sex with grown men. By the time I turned 15, I would secretly wish to be raped so I can feel alive. Crazy, I know.

After enduring one abusive situation after another, I just wanted out. Out meaning permanently gone from this earth or out by running away. It was touch and go for a while. It could have gone either way. But eventually, I chose to run away. So, I worked my part-time job trying to save my money but couldn't. My mom took my paycheck to pay bills. I always wondered did she know I was planning to leave. But fortunately, my stepfather left before I could finish high school when I was 17 and I thought things were going to get better. I started dating Wayne who was 23 and a custodian at my part-time job. I revealed that I was going into the military, and soon after, he asked me to get married. After all the abuse to my body, mind, and spirit...maybe this was the way to happiness. I told my mom and my uncle of our plans. My mom didn't say anything. My uncle couldn't stand him. He told me not to marry him because he was a leech. But I wasn't listening to any of that. But I wasn't listening to any of that. So less than a year later, I'm 18, married, and now in the military. I decided to go into the military as Security Police because my recruiter told me I only had 2 choices: I can be a Law Enforcement Officer (they patrolled the base) or I can be a Security Police (they patrolled the planes and the missiles). My dumb ass believed him...not knowing any better. I found out later there was a huge push to put women into the police field due to a lawsuit. My scores were good enough to do almost anything. But I saw the weapons that I could learn to shoot...so I chose to be Security Police.

My first duty station was Minot, North Dakota as Security Police guarding missile silos. This meant,

I was the only female in the flight of over 100 men. I had to go into the field with a crew of 8 men. Our rotation was a grueling: three days in the missile field, travel back to the base on the 4th day, off for three days, then one training day, and then back to the missile field. Being a Missile cop, meant everyone carried 6 magazines that carried 30 rounds per magazine. A magazine in the chamber at all times. So, you are locked and loaded at all times. My first partner put me in a "fuck or fight" position. Being that I wasn't a fighter, I had to fuck. This went on about six months. Then he left to go to another base. Thank God. Then I got paired with another partner. He was crazy but he didn't want anything from me. He was a breath of fresh air.

By this time the newly wed euphoria had worn off, and I was growing tired of carry all the bills with no help in site from Wayne. I finally had to admit that my uncle was right: my husband was a leech.

We argued constantly, especially when I returned from field duty because he refused to get a job.

Things went from sugar to shit real fast when I got called to the commanders' office due to being delinquent on paying a bill. It turned out that my husband had forged my name on a lease to own boom box radio and hadn't paid a dime. I was immediately reprimanded even though you can clearly see that II was in the field when this purchase was made. This particular reprimand was closely equivalent to being put on a Performance Improvement Plan and this strike is now part of my permanent record. In the military, you are responsible for your dependents' actions.

My commander was a raciest, sexist, asshole. Even after I proved the lease was forged, he didn't care; he was determined to push me towards being discharge. In his mind, women didn't belong in *his* military, and being both Black and a woman made me a prime target. I could see my days were numbered.

I decided to divorce Wayne. If I was going to be discharged, I wanted it to be for something I actually did wrong. Plus, I had secretly started dating my soon-to-be baby's father, Davis. While I was out in the field, Wayne packed up his things—and some of mine—and left, taking my car with him. Not long after Wayne left, my mom passed away, and then I discovered I was pregnant with Davis's child. In the voice of Momma Dee…"and in that order!"

After my mom passed, I was ordered to see a psychiatrist - thank God for him. He already my commander's reputation for being a sexist, racist asshole. My psychiatrist saw that I was at my breaking point. He arranged for me to be transferred out from under that commander's and had me reassigned to a role that didn't require carrying a weapon. He felt that I was going to hurt someone or hurt myself. I was truly in a dark space.

When I first felt my baby move, everything became real. That moment gave me the reason I needed to live. I realized that I now had a responsibility to give my baby the best life possible. I finally felt a purpose, and with that, I started working on putting my mind in a better place.

You'd think things were finally getting better. Wrong! Just when I needed support the most, the father of my child decided he didn't want to be a father. I was devastated. I grew up without my father, and I'd always promised myself that if I had a child, she would grow up with both parents. I never imagined he wouldn't want to be there for her. Despite the verbal, mental, and physical abuse, I convinced myself that all he needed was to see his child being born—then he would love her. I convinced myself to stay, telling myself that if he could see his child being born and still not love her, then I would leave. Sadly, that moment came, and I had to move on.

I left for my next duty station at Anderson Air Force Base in Guam, while Davis was sent to Korea. After about a year, Davis decided to leave the military and suddenly wanted to get married. Stupid me, I ended a healthy, loving relationship—the best I'd ever had at that point— to marry him. I convinced myself that this was my chance to create a real family for my child with her father. Let me add, the relationship that I decided to end was the first healthy relationship I've had, at that point. He truly loved me. But someone that really never experienced what real love was…didn't know what I had. I truly regretted hurting him. But at the time, I felt I had to try and make it work with my baby's father. So, I married him.

Our marital bliss lasted about three months... if that... and that verbally, mentally, and physically abusive man was back. Now, I realized that I made a mistake. It got to the point that I didn't want to have sex with him. But he quickly reminded me of my duties as a wife. So I decided to just lay there and not move while he was having sex. I felt like Celie from The Color Purple, and he was Mister. I just laid there like a corpse while he did his business. I watched the clock praying for it to be over soon. He didn't care. He did what he needed then rolled off of me. Then I turned on the TV. That was my life.

Finally, I was sick and tired of being sick and tired. I knew in my heart that God had something better for me and my daughter. I FINALLY started to realize that I deserved better that what I've been getting. I could not allow my child to grow up in this condition believing that this was healthy.

He flew into a rage, jumping on me and choking me until I was on the brink of unconsciousness. Then, he abruptly released me. Then he started cursing me out and calling me every name he could think of but a child of God. Then he reveals he had a girlfriend and was ready to leave anyway. It was very terrifying but yet, I felt a strange sense of liberation. I felt like I had finally taken some control over my life.

I let the miliary know that we are divorcing, and they started the process of him moving back to continental United States. He moved out.

Now that you are caught up…this is what happened…

The summer of '91 was a turning point in my life. I had gone to the movies with a "so-called" girlfriend and a male friend, expecting a fun and carefree outing. Little did I know, that day would mark the end of my time as a victim. After having such a great time at the movies, my male friend suggested that we go grab something to eat. My girlfriend said that she needed to go. So my male friend said that he would drop me off at home. My stupid ass agreed.

Now, remember Davis said he had a girlfriend. By this time, we had already signed the divorce papers. All we were just waiting on was for it to be presented before a judge. I'm thinking life is finally good.

I'm sitting at a table at a local eatery with my male friend kee-keeing having the time of my life. He grabs my hand, turning on the charm to the max. I'm sitting there, googly-eyed, completely captivated by him—when, out of the corner of my eye, I see someone in the background rushing toward our table. And before I could truly comprehend what was really going on…my soon-to-be ex-husband Davis came over the back of my male friend and started choking me…like he's done several times before. This time, I truly believed he was going to kill me. In what felt like hours, but was really just a split second, a thought flashed through my mind: *"Are you really going to let this man kill you? Will your child be raised in foster care? No one in your family will take her, and you know his family won't take her. You are all she has. Are you going to fight to live, or just let go and die?"* My answer was clear: *"I'm going to fight to live!"*

At that moment, I turned into another person and had an out of body experience. It was my body…but that wasn't me. This new me found strength that I didn't know I had. The new me gave Davis a couple of two-pieces and several biscuits aka combination of punches that rocked him so hard…it brought him down to his knees. Then I turned and grabbed one of the iron chairs and started the motion to hit Davis while he was down and my male friend reached out, grabbing the chair and shouting, *"You're going to kill him!"* I snapped out of it, regaining my senses. As I looked around, I noticed everyone in the restaurant was pressed against the walls, watching in stunned silence. Davis, now shirtless, stumbled to his feet and quickly ran out the door. My male friend grabbed me, and we rushed to his car, speeding away from the scene.

Davis was banned from the base. I got restricted to the base. This was their way of keeping us separated. They gave Davis an expressed one-way ticket off the island of Guam. It wasn't until many years later that I found out it was my so-called girlfriend who had told Davis where I was and who I was with.

But that was the last day I stopped being a victim. I realized I deserved better, for the sake of my daughter. From that moment on, I refused to let anyone talk crazy to me or abuse me—verbally, mentally, or physically.

Now, for transparency…I would admit, I went from being docile to taking the "fuck with me if you want to" attitude. I started to get into trouble. If you even thought about crossing me…you felt my wrath.

That one summer day in '91 was the last day I was sick and tired of being sick and tired. I stopped being a victim. I made a vow to never let anyone make me feel unworthy, and I kept that promise. It took a lot of counseling—both self-guided and professional—to find a healthy balance. Now, five husbands later, I finally feel like I have a partner who respects me and accepts me with all my mistakes and flaws, just as I am.

From Hardship to Hope by Kyon Edwards

Growing up in the early '80s was a mix of the best and worst times of my life. On one hand, it was a time of carefree living, not worrying about anything, and not stressing over where my next meal would come from. But looking back now, I realize it was also some of the hardest times. I was born in Hopkins Park, Illinois, a small town where dirt and gravel roads were still the norm. My mom had five children, and there was no father figure in the house.

We lived in what could only be described as unfit homes. I remember one house we called "the chicken coop." It was truly a disaster—holes in the walls, a kitchen that had been burned, and an electrical fire from the switch for the outside light. Raccoons somehow managed to get inside, though we never figured out how. We had no running water, so we had to go outside and pump water just to cook or bathe. And there was no heat, so we had to rely on a wood-burning stove to keep warm. We all slept in the front room because it was the only room warm enough to sleep in.

That was one of the many houses we lived in, and as an adult, I now realize just how unfit it was to live in. But what's more, I remember another house that I thought was a major step up from the first. It was a beautiful 3-bedroom home with lots of land, and for a while, everything seemed normal—until one day, one of us saw a snake crawling down the hallway.

We all ran out of the house, except for my youngest sister. Standing outside, we yelled through the window for her to get out because there was a snake in the hallway. When she heard us, she looked back down the hallway, saw the snake, and immediately jumped out the window. When my mom got home, she asked why we were all outside. We explained, and she decided not to go back in until her boyfriend arrived. He went inside to search for the snake, eventually finding it in the kitchen, near the sink where the pots and pans were stored. It had crawled into a jar, and he managed to pick it up with a stick and take it outside. He shot the snake once he was sure it was secure.

For a while, we didn't see any more snakes, but soon, they started popping up randomly around the house. It got so bad that we eventually had to move.

Before we moved, I remember my mom's boyfriend at the time going into the crawl space. The door to it was on the outside of the house, and when he opened it and turned on his flashlight, all we could see were snakes—like a snake den down there. It was terrifying.

At the time, I didn't fully understand that we were struggling and very poor. Being the youngest of five, I always got the hand-me-downs from my older siblings. It was just the way things were, and

I never questioned it. But looking back now, I can see how much we were just getting by.

Fast forward a few years, and we eventually found a house that was actually worth living in. Things were going well for a while, but then my mom suddenly got sick. One day, the ambulance had to come and take her because she couldn't get out of bed. We didn't know what was wrong with her at the time.

The next morning, my grandmother came to take my two older sisters, leaving me and my older brother at the house. I was 13, and he was 15. A few hours passed, and we were doing our usual—bothering each other—when the phone rang. My brother picked it up, and while he was talking to whoever was on the other end, I was still messing around.

Then, he sat down and started crying. It stopped me in my tracks, and I immediately wanted to know what was wrong. When he hung up the phone, he started crying even harder. I asked him what happened, and through his tears, he told me that Mama was dead. I couldn't fully process it, but I started crying, too—though mostly because I saw him so upset.

Life after that moment was never the same. Racism is another traumatic reality I've had to face. If a Black person ever tells you they've never experienced racism, I will argue that they've likely masked it, locked it away in their mind, and thrown away the key. Let me share an experience I had, as well as one my son went through.

I was going to high school in an all-white town, and as a kid, you knew racism existed, but if it didn't directly affect you, you didn't pay much attention to it. One day, some friends and I stayed after school and went to a basketball court in a predominantly white neighborhood. Time passed, and it started getting dark. Out of nowhere, about five police cars pulled up to us, acting like we had just committed a crime or broken out of jail.

The officers rushed up and asked what we were doing there. It was obvious we were teenagers, just playing basketball. They then asked how we were getting home. We told them one of our parents would be coming to pick us up. Instead of letting us wait for our ride, they told us to get in the back of their cars and drove us down a dark, isolated dirt road.

As a child who had watched *Roots* and countless other movies about Black history, I knew that getting put in the back of a police car only meant one of two things: jail or worse—getting beaten or killed. My heart started racing as the police sped down that dark road. Then, without warning, they stopped at a remote spot in my town, told us all to get out, and sped off. We were left standing there, and we had to walk about two miles or more to get home.

That was one of the scariest moments of my life. Years later, my son had his own encounter with police that still haunts me. He was coming home from school on his bike when suddenly, the police sped up and cut right in front of him, trying to stop him or even make him flip over the hood of their car. They jumped out, rushed him, and started asking who he was and where he was coming from because he "fit the description" of someone they were looking for. They then took his backpack off and began searching through it without permission.

Being just a child on his own, he didn't know his rights and was too scared to say anything. As a Black father, I was beyond angry and upset that my son had to go through that. But it also made me sit him down and explain something I never wanted to have to explain to a 12-year-old: that there are people out there who will hate him simply because of the color of his skin—not because of his character, not because of anything he has done wrong, but just because of the way he looks. That moment, for me, was heartbreaking, but it was a harsh reality I had to prepare him for.

Reflecting on my life, I've endured poverty, loss, fear, and injustice. Yet, through it all, I've discovered resilience and the importance of equipping the next generation to face the realities of the world. These experiences have shaped me but do not define me. Instead, they've strengthened my resolve, deepened my awareness, and fueled my commitment to breaking cycles of hardship for my family. Moments like these have molded my perspective, teaching me the power of perseverance while revealing the harsh truths of being Black in America. Even so, I hold steadfastly to hope and faith, believing that no matter the challenges, we have the strength to rise above.

A Girlhood Promise by Yanique McKoy

Girlhood lies in that fragile space between childhood and womanhood. A time when possibilities seem endless, and hope can feel as real as the air you breathe. But for me, girlhood felt like a half-written chapter torn out of my story before it even began. My early years were spent navigating various home environments scarred by violence, alcoholism, and abandonment. I learned early that promises were cheap, and protection was a myth. The adults I depended on were too busy fighting their own battles to care much about mine. The only person I could depend on was me.

At 11 years-old my mother's long-term boyfriend tried to stab her. That night I stopped being a little girl. I remember hearing yelling and then a high-pitched scream catapulted me from the couch to their bedroom door. I saw the glint of the knife and the wildness in his eyes as he lunged for her face. The thudding in my chest felt like a drumbeat only I could hear. I began screaming and threatened to call the police. My presence provided my mom enough distraction to escape. Their relationship continued in this topsy turvy fashion for a few more years. At the onset of every fight, I remembered the vow I made to myself at 11—one whispered and etched in the far reaches of my subconscious: this would never be me.

I poured everything into high school, determined to prove that I was just as smart and capable, as my cousins and classmates. When it came time for college, I went as far from home as I could, craving a fresh start and eager to write my own story. By the time Christmas break rolled around freshman year, I was excited to reconnect with my friends back home and swap stories of our college escapades. So, when one of my closest friends invited me along to meet a guy she'd been talking to, I was all in. She didn't want to go alone for their first meeting, and I was game for the adventure. He brought his cousin along, so I wouldn't feel like a third wheel. We met up at a local bowling alley. When we walked in there they were, two guys each around six feet tall and well dressed. Anticipation and excitement flowed between us. Introductions were quick and the night flowed effortlessly. We laughed until our sides hurt, shared stories, and flirted in the casual, familiar way you do when you're young and the night feels endless. By the time the bowling alley was closing, CJ, the cousin, asked for my number.

He called me the very next day and we spent three hours talking on the phone. Our conversation shifted easily from one thing to the next. CJ was 24, just starting his career, and I peppered him with questions: What was work like? What did he do for fun? Why was he single? We teased each other mercilessly about our bowling "skills," and laughed about events of the prior night. CJ had an air of confidence that I found intriguing. Before we ended our call, we made plans to go to the movies and dinner. For the next three weeks, we darted around the city eating, shopping, ice skating and getting to know each other. By the time I returned to school, we agreed to have a long-distance relationship.

CJ and I kept up our nightly calls, each one stretching long into the early morning. Between classes, social clubs, my part-time job, and friends, he became the constant I looked forward to each night. By the time summer break arrived, I was practically counting down the days until I could see him again.

The moment I got home, he showed up at my mom's door with a bouquet so large I could barely see his face behind it. He insisted I wear something nice for dinner because he made reservations at my favorite restaurant. After dinner, we headed back to his apartment, in a well-off part of the city. His place was sleek, stylish, and definitely pricey. I couldn't help but wonder how someone his age afforded all this, an upscale apartment, the expensive car and the high-end clothes. He made some offhand comments about where his money came from, but they sounded more like wild stories than reality. He joked about girls working in strip clubs for him or his dad being a well-to-do hustler, but I brushed them off. Sure, there were pieces that didn't fully add up, but he didn't act like the dope boys I'd grown up around, and he definitely didn't come across as some spoiled kid living off his parents' money. I figured in time he would trust me with the truth.

The summer continued with impromptu dates, hanging with friends and an industry internship with a major television network. To celebrate a friend's birthday, all of my girls decided to go to the club. We made plans in the week and each prepared for our Saturday night of fun. Saturday morning, I woke up determined to get the final touches for my outfit. I didn't want to wear something I had worn several times before. CJ and I met at the mall, and we ended up spending the day together. We shopped and ate and cruised around the city. We went back to his apartment in the late evening. We hung out for an hour before I need to leave and get ready to go out.

I began gathering my things and told him I would be leaving to meet up with my friends. As I approached the door of his bedroom, he blocked my ability to exit by placing his back against the door. I passionately kissed him and reached for the doorknob. He grasped the knob before I could reach it and told me I couldn't leave. I smiled at him and said why not. He told me I couldn't leave without sleeping with him. I told him I would come back after the club and spend the night with him. I again reach for the door, and he batted by hand down. In a stern voice, he told me no woman of his is allowed to go to the club without sleeping with him first. I tried again to open the door, but his solid frame didn't budge. Instead, he lifted me up and threw me on the bed. The dress I wore rode up my thighs as I scooted away. He grabbed my legs and dragged me underneath him. I tried to keep moving hoping to release the hold he had on me. His body weight was suffocating me, and I begged for a release that never came. I told him I would start screaming, but he told me no one would hear. I felt him rip my underwear and realized there was nothing I could do to keep the inevitable from happening. I pleaded with him to use a condom, but he put his hand around my throat and told me to stop moving. No amount of begging, pleading or crying could change my fate. Acceptance of my circumstance paralyzed me. Tears blurred my vision, and I disassociated from my body. I froze in place waiting for him to finish. When he was done, he climbed out of the bed and stood over me. His six-foot-tall frame imposing over my 5'3 stature. He smirked and said, "now you can go to the club." I hurriedly gathered my things and rushed out of his apartment.

Shaken by what transpired, I called my cousin and recounted what CJ had done. She asked me if I wanted to call the police, but I said no. What would I tell them? How would I prove that I wasn't a willing participant in an act we had performed countless times together before tonight. It would be his word against mine. On the drive home, I replayed the day in my mind, searching for where it had taken such a dark, unexpected turn. Just hours earlier, we'd been lost in our usual easy banter, but somehow, things had spiraled into something I could never have imagined. Something that left me feeling shattered and betrayed. I couldn't understand how it happened, how he had gone from being someone I trusted to violating me in the worst way. I couldn't put the pieces of the puzzle together.

I had successfully ignored CJ's calls and messages for a week before he showed up at my mom's house. Not wanting to arise my mother's suspicion, I agreed to go out with CJ. My mom and I had never been close, and I knew I wouldn't find support in her. Her judgement in relationships had always been poor. So, the less she knew about our situation the better. CJ presented me with flowers, a giant teddy bear and an apology card. We sat in the parking lot of TGI Friday's as he expressed his regret. "I don't know what came over me," he pleaded. "I got carried away and I'm sorry." With tears in his eyes, he continued to beg for my forgiveness. After a few weeks of him showering me with adoration, I relented and began calling him again. We easily fell back into our old routine. I made it a point not to tell anyone, other than my cousin, what had happened.

As the end of summer approached, I found myself busy getting ready to head back to school. CJ, however, wanted me to spend every possible moment with him. After a long day of picking up necessities for school, I made my way over to his place, eager to relax. When I walked in, he was in the middle of a heated debate with one of his friends. It seemed harmless at first, the kind of argument that could've gone either way. CJ looked at me and asked my opinion. "Tell me, does ketchup belong in the fridge or the pantry?" Without hesitation, I laughed and said, "Fridge, of course." Before I could explain why, CJ's friend laughed, pointing at him. "See? I told you, nigga. You want to keep that shit in the hot ass pantry," he said, continuing to laugh. CJ's face darkened, and he turned to his friend, snapping, "Shut the fuck up." His friend just chuckled, raising his hands. "Hey, you're the one who thinks that makes sense. You should shut up." I could feel the tension simmering, so I tried to keep it light. "It's not that big a deal," I said. "Ketchup can go in either place, really." CJ shot me a hard look and set his gun on the counter. "Let this be the last time you side with another nigga over me." His tone cut through the room, and his friend muttered, "Chill, man, it's just ketchup." But CJ's anger didn't stop. He turned on me, his voice rising, each word sharper than the last. I barely had time to process what was happening before he grabbed me by the jaw, his fingers pressing into my cheeks. Glaring into my eyes, he said, "I don't take disrespect from bitches." I twisted free, heart racing, and grabbed the few things I'd left in his room. Without another word, I made my way to the front door. Suddenly, I felt a pull on my arm and hair before the wall came crashing into my face. CJ had slammed me headfirst into the wall and my body slid to the floor. By the time I got up off the floor, CJ's friend stood between us. He mouthed for me to leave, while trying to calm CJ down. While scraping my belongings off the floor, I released a tirade of my thoughts. I told CJ that only a weak man would put his hands on a woman and to forget that he ever met me. With the adrenaline flowing through my body, I didn't initially feel the pain from the knot forming on my head. When I walked out of that apartment I never looked back. I didn't answer any of his phone calls. Returning to school helped put distance between us and allowed me to avoid the questioning probes about our relationship status from my friends and family.

I never spoke about those seven months with CJ, not about the assaults, the manipulation, or the slow erosion of who I thought I was. That relationship left me riddled with guilt and shame, a haunting sense that I had somehow failed myself. How could I have missed the signs? I'd grown up surrounded by men like him, seen this kind of violence up close. I'd promised myself at eleven years old that I'd never let anyone hurt me like that. And yet, when the first assault happened, I ignored my instincts and let it slide. I was ashamed that I stayed, that I'd let someone tear me down piece by piece. Since I was a child, I trusted my intuition, I was a good judge of character, too sharp to end up in a relationship like this. And maybe that's what hurt the most, that I'd betrayed the very trust I'd built in myself. For fifteen years, that shame kept me silent.

At 33, after a series of unshakable panic attacks, I finally decided to go to therapy. The weight of countless traumas had become impossible to ignore, I felt like I was unraveling. During my first session, as I recounted one painful memory after another, my therapist paused, observing me carefully. She noted how detached I seemed, how

I described horrific experiences as casually as listing items on a grocery list.

For years, I'd taught myself to compartmentalize my pain, to protect myself from vulnerability. I thought silence would keep me safe. But in therapy, I began to see that my silence hadn't protected me. It had given these memories a quiet, insidious power over my life. Little by little, I realized that healing meant facing each story, each wound, without hiding from the emotions beneath. I had to rediscover how to connect with my emotions, set boundaries for the how I wanted to live my life and eliminate the people and things that no longer served me. I had long learned not to ignore my instincts and emotionally detached from people quite easily. But now being in a stable relationship, these trauma responses no longer benefitted me, and I had to learn to let them go. My brain was used to chaos and struggled to cope in a world free of disfunction. Waiting for the other shoe to drop kept me from being fully present in my life and experiencing what a loving relationship felt like.

Every day, I committed to an emotional check-in, a moment to name my feelings and let them hold space in my body or surrender them to a higher power. Slowly, I learned to forgive those who had hurt me, including CJ. I came to understand that forgiveness wasn't a gift for them, it was a release for me. I wanted to clear space in my heart to experience the richness life had to offer, unburdened by resentment. I realized that if I held onto bitterness for every wrong done to me, there'd be no room left for joy, hope, or possibility.

Over time, I have come to believe that we're all flawed in some way and, deep down, most of us want forgiveness when we stumble and cause harm. At least that is my hope. Healing helped create a determination in me to walk through life reclaiming the power I once lost, to live fully in the abundance that each new day brings.

Sometimes, I still think back on my choices and wish some things had turned out differently. But I understand now that every experience, both the painful and the beautiful, have shaped me into the person I am.

The Triumph of Saving My Marriage: A Journey of Faith, Healing, and Restoration by ANONYMOUS 1

Our journey began with a leap of faith. After years of moving from state to state, searching for stability, my wife and I felt a pull toward Georgia. We hoped it would be a place where we could rebuild our lives and heal the wounds that had been weighing us down. A friend offered us a temporary place to stay—a blessing we believed was part of God's provision. Little did we know, the path ahead would test our faith in ways we couldn't have imagined.

Upon arriving, we faced immediate challenges. We were still navigating the fragile process of reconciliation after mistakes I had made in our relationship. I carried guilt and a deep desire to make things right. I believed that by working hard and securing jobs, we could lay a new foundation. But doors didn't open as quickly as we hoped. My wife felt called to deepen her spiritual journey, focusing on healing and counseling through our friend's home-based church. She told me she believed God wanted her to take this path, which meant not seeking employment at that time.

As I took on extra work to support us, the weight grew heavier. I didn't fully understand her decision, and frustration began to seep into my spirit. But amid the struggle, I held onto my faith, praying for guidance and trusting that God had a plan—even if I couldn't see it yet.

We finally saved enough to secure our own apartment, only to discover the night before moving in that it was uninhabitable. This setback felt crushing. I questioned why these obstacles kept arising when we were trying so hard. But in those moments of despair, I remembered Proverbs 3:5-6: "Trust in the Lord with all your

heart and lean not on your own understanding."
Perhaps there was a reason we couldn't see.
Returning to our friend's home intensified
tensions. Misunderstandings and frustrations led
to conflicts that tested our patience and grace. I
found myself withdrawing, leaning more on
unhealthy coping mechanisms than on prayer and
faith. Yet, even then, God was working on my
heart, gently nudging me back toward Him.

When my wife became pregnant, it added both joy
and complexity to our situation. Feeling
overwhelmed, I decided it was time to solidify our
commitment before God and marry her. We had a
spiritual ceremony, placing our marriage in God's
hands without the legal formalities. I believed that
by honoring God first, He would honor our
union.

But the road remained rocky. Financial strains and
personal conflicts continued to challenge us. Then
came the most painful trial: my wife felt led to
take a break from our marriage to pursue what she

believed was God's calling. She became involved with another man, and I was left grappling with heartache and confusion. It was during this darkest hour that I fell to my knees, crying out to God for strength, wisdom, and healing.

Psalm 34:18 says, "The Lord is close to the brokenhearted and saves those who are crushed in spirit." I clung to this promise. I immersed myself in prayer, seeking God's will above my own desires. Through His grace, I began to find peace amid the chaos. I worked on myself—spiritually, emotionally, and physically—trusting that God was molding me for a purpose.

Caring for our children became my primary focus. I wanted to provide them with love and stability, reflecting God's unconditional love for us. Friends and spiritual mentors surrounded me, offering support and reminding me that God's plans are always for our good, even when we can't see the bigger picture.

One evening, as my wife and I prayed over our daughter—a practice we had not done together in some time—the presence of the Holy Spirit filled the room. Walls we'd built between us started to crumble. We confessed our hurts, forgave each other, and allowed God's healing power to begin restoring our relationship. It was a profound reminder that "with God all things are possible" (Matthew 19:26).

Our reconciliation wasn't instantaneous, but it was genuine. We started rebuilding our marriage on the solid rock of faith, recognizing that without Abba at the center, our efforts would be in vain. We began attending church together, studying the Word, and seeking counsel from faith leaders who supported our journey.

Today, our marriage is a testament to Our Heavenly Father's incredible mercy and grace. We're not perfect, and challenges still arise, but we face them together, anchored in our faith. We pray together, laugh together, and support each other's callings. I've learned to appreciate her spiritual gifts, and she's embraced my role as a provider and protector of our family.

To anyone facing trials in their marriage or personal life, I want to offer this encouragement: God's love is relentless, and His grace is sufficient for every weakness. When the storms of life rage, and the path seems uncertain, remember that God is our refuge and strength, an ever-present help in trouble (Psalm 46:1). Surrender your struggles to Him and allow His peace to fill your heart.

Today, we are stronger together. Life isn't perfect, but it's real, grounded in understanding and grace. Our journey taught me that even in the darkest times, there is always hope. Grace and forgiveness can create bridges over the deepest divides, and if we are willing to see past our pain and look toward healing, there is a path forward. Trust in our Heavenly Father's timing, lean on His Word, and don't lose hope. "And we know that in all things God works for the good of those who love

Him, who have been called according to His purpose" (Romans 8:28).

Our story is one of redemption and the miraculous power of God's love. I pray that it inspires you to hold on to faith, seek God's guidance, and believe that restoration is possible. No matter how deep the hurt or how great the divide, God's healing hands can reach you.

Our lives are woven with second chances, not just to rebuild relationships, but to grow into people of strength and compassion. So, keep going. There is hope, and you will find it—often in the most unexpected places.

Through Zay Zay's Eyes: A Story of Love, Loss, and Resilience by P.P.

I imagined growing up as a child thinking life would be perfect. However, Mom worked three jobs, so we never really saw her, and Dad worked overnight, which meant he slept through the day. Being the youngest by 11 years, my sisters and brother felt more like my guardians. By the time I was coming up, they already had their own lives, so childhood often felt very lonely.

Growing up in the 90s was pretty lit, though. We came and went without the constant obligation to technology like kids have today. I had a handful of neighborhood friends, and everybody looked out for each other.

My brother, Zay Zay, was like my rock. From the stories I've heard, he was the handsome kid every girl liked. He played football and had a job, which, in the Black community at the time, brought a lot of jealousy his way.

He was my protector from the beginning.

I vividly remember one Fourth of July when I wanted to go outside to watch fireworks with my friends. Of course, it was dark, and my dad was strict about being out past the streetlights. He didn't care what was going on. As a child, I was subtly rebellious, which often resulted in many ass whooping's.

On this particular holiday I felt extremely courageous and asked to go outside. When he said, "**NO**" I yelled, "**WELL I'M GOING TO JUMP OUT THE WINDOW!**" Before I could even think about what I just said, my dad already had the belt in his hand. As frightening as this may sound to children of today, this is a very teachable and special moment to me. My brother, Zay Zay, stepped in like a knight in shining armor, jumping between us to protect me from our father, who was much bigger than the both of us. This moment showed just how far Zay Zay would go to protect his little sister.

After that day, I never disrespected my dad in such a manner again. That was probably the last ass whooping I ever received, and I can truly say, **I LEARNED THAT DAY.**

Oh, how I wish I could have protected my brother from this mean, cold world—especially from drugs.

Over time, I became more reclused as a child, for no particular reason. Maybe that's just who I was meant to be. During this period of my life, my mom went to jail, my brother became more distant, and my sisters had their own lives. I had no clue; I was just being a kid. I had no control.

I started noticing Zay Zay acting even more distant and not like himself. At times, it almost scared me to be around him. Eventually, my mom sent me to live with another family. They became an extension of my own family, loving me as if I were their own. While I gained so much from this experience, it taught me that life is fragile—like a bubble that can pop at any moment.

Most of my good core memories came from living with this family. I learned a lot and made friends with the kids they babysat. But at the end of the day, when the other kids went home to their families, it was just me. Where was my family? I still got every opportunity to be with them, but I wanted to **BE WITH THEM** like most normal folks. I don't resent this time in my life, because it made me who I am, but there was always a missing component.

By this point, Zay Zay was in and out of group homes. Seeing him like this broke my heart. Eventually, I learned the truth—my precious brother marijuana that was laced in the early 2000s. I knew something was wrong, but I didn't KNOW. I wasn't a very inquisitive child, but I paid attention.

This was a heavy and critical lesson to learn so early in life. I never bothered with any type of drug until much later on in my life due to this reason. My first usage with marijuana was a pleasant memory, but it could've went far left had I gotten around the wrong crowd or let it become an addiction. Luckily for me today, and let's face it, these drugs in the streets are not what they use to be.

As much as we loved Zay Zay, he had become too dangerous. It had become a disease—a mental illness. It was like a light switch being turned off, especially if he did not take medications. Even if he did, he was just not the same.

Over the years, I watched the toll this took on my family. Zay Zay was in and out of jail for crimes committed against others. As I've grown older and now have a child of my own, I want him to be a part of my life. I often wonder what life could have been like if things had been different. This part of me has left an extremely traumatic impression on my scope of life because now it seems it's like he never existed.

I deal with this trauma by staying true to who I am and knowing my limits when engaging with certain crowds. One of my greatest gifts is my intuition— I can sense when a situation or crowd isn't right for me. Of all the things I love about myself, I'm proud that I'm not easily led astray. Not to say that Zay Zay wasn't, but unfortunately bad things happen. I do my best to avoid such situations, because not everyone is your friend and not everyone can be trusted.

Being aware of the devastating effects of drugs has always been a blessing. Statistics show that 8.3 million Americans suffer from an illicit drug use disorder. Of the 21 million Americans who have at least one addiction, only 10% receive treatment. Additionally, 53% of drug abusers also have a mental illness.

In Zay Zay's case, he used maybe a handful of times, received treatment, but it effected his entire life. He could have been anybody, and this thought haunts me.
Sometimes, I imagine what life could have been like for him. Although his experience didn't happen directly to me, it impacted my life in more

ways than one could comprehend like a domino effect. I chose every day to live above this traumatic experience and love through him.

Brotherhood and Betrayal by ANONYMOUS 2

Back in my New York days, I was no stranger to gang life. It wasn't just a choice—it was a lifestyle, a bond I thought was unbreakable. But when a gang mission took a turn, I found myself leaving and starting fresh in Georgia. Not long after I arrived, I connected with a crew from the same set I was with back home.

We were supposed to be brothers, united by a code that ran deeper than blood. It was about loyalty, trust, and holding each other down, no matter what. Or so I thought.

So later on, I ended up getting into a problem (over a female of course...lol) with another gang —a Spanish set. In my mind, I'm the toughest, the rawest G nigga to walk the earth. Whether its three niggas or thirty niggas, it doesn't matter to me. I lived by the code: *If you come for me, you better be ready to die—because I am.*

That mindset was my armor, my shield against the world. But it also blinded me to the cracks in the foundation of this so-called brotherhood I had built my life around.

I do see now I was in the wrong because I had slept with this guy's girlfriend. But at the time, my thought process was…that was *his* girl, which meant *his* problem. So, we ended up getting into it at a bus stop and I put the beats on him. I mean really bad.

The next day, I heard that he and his gang were out looking for me—and they had guns. So, in true ignorant fashion, I decided I needed to get my hands on a gun too. That way, I could find them first and handle the situation before they got to me.

I asked a family friend for his father's gun. We were around the same age, and he knew exactly what I was planning. He agreed to get it to me. But instead, he betrayed me by telling his father. His father was furious and ended up telling my mother. Now, my entire family knew about my reckless plan, and they were rightfully angry.

We shared a mutual friend. And told the mutual friend that if he brings that nigga around me, I'm going to beat the shit out of him. It was an "On Sight" situation, and he agreed that we needed some time to cool off.

A week later, this mutual friend came to my house and said that there were a lot of women at the pool and my whole crew was out there. I said I was about to eat but would be out in a few. I then invited him to eat with my family, which he accepted. After we ate, we went out to the pool where that same family friend was, and they both surrounded me, ready to fight. I never left the house without a weapon, so I went into full attack mode, stabbed the family friend, and put the knife to his neck, saying, "If you even blink, I will Nicole Simpson your ass!" I realized what I was doing and let him go, then walked away.

They ended up calling the cops, and a warrant was issued for my arrest on attempted murder charges. I turned myself in and spent 30 days in jail on a $75,000 bail. When I got out, I was told I was facing 15-25 years in prison. At the time, I was in my early 20s. I was devastated. My mom told me I needed to go to college. She thought that if the judge saw I was trying to change my life, he might give me a lighter sentence. So, I enrolled in community college.

That's where I met a white guy who changed the course of my life. I can't remember his name, but he asked me for a cigarette, so I gave him one. He noticed I was quiet and asked if I was okay. I told him I was fine, just dealing with some heavy shit. He said, "Talk to me, I'm all ears." I explained the situation to him, and he gave me the name of a lawyer who had recently gotten a guy off who bashed a cop's head in with the hood of his car.

I met with the lawyer, and he took my case and got my discovery. He asked me if my friends were really my friends. I said definitely, and then he handed me a packet, saying, "I'm not supposed to let you see this until we're at trial, but you trusted me by telling me you were guilty, so I'm trusting you." I opened it and saw that every member of my gang at the time had written a statement against me to the police. I was heartbroken and angry.

I told the girl I was dating at the time about the betrayal, and she confirmed my suspicions. She said they were no good and had tried to sleep with her while I was in jail because they thought I'd never get out. She admitted she hadn't told me because she didn't want me to violate the conditions of my bond.

I was already in the process of changing, praying, and talking to God. My lawyer knew the District Attorney personally and had lunch with him. On the first day of court, he asked me if I trusted him, and I said, of course. He said, "Whatever they ask you, say yes." I said, "I got you."

I went in, and the judge asked, "Are you guilty of the charges?" I said, "Yes, sir." He asked, "Do you agree to the plea agreement?" I said, "Yes, sir." He said, "Okay, hopefully, you learned to choose your friends better. You have pleaded guilty to the lesser charge of affray, you will do 6 months of probation, and a $300 dollar fine, and you are to not step foot in the area."

It all took place for 5 years. I was so happy I cried and promised myself and God I would never pick up a flag or be quick to anger.

Now, I still struggle with anger to this day, but I keep my composure to honor that promise. The white guy who gave me the lawyer, I never saw again. I wanted to thank him and tell him what happened, but no one knew who I was talking about. When I asked around, it was like he didn't exist. I have never seen or heard from him since... who do you think that was?

Now my friends are all upstanding men. My life in the streets is over. I'm a father now, and I have so much to live for. **I owe it all to God.**

I would have gotten out on June 25, 2024, had I gone to jail.

The Smile is The Scar by Dethra U. Giles

We sat around the table—a familiar circle of middle-aged friends, laughing and reconnecting as though it hadn't been months since our last gathering. There was a warmth and ease in the room, the kind that can only be found among people who've known each other long enough to skip the pleasantries and dive into the depths. Conversation flowed, touching on the highs and lows of our lives, and, inevitably, the question of life trauma was posed.

The question made its way around the table, each friend taking a turn to share a burden or a memory. When it skipped over me, I didn't mind; reliving my trauma isn't exactly on my list of go-to topics for a lighthearted night out with friends. But before the conversation could move forward, someone turned, meeting my eyes with a gentle, probing look. "And you, Dethra. You've never really had any trauma, have you? I mean, your life… it always looks like nothing major or life altering has gone wrong."

I felt the familiar stretch of my lips into a smile— the same one I've worn in the face of every challenge, every memory, every heartache. "Everyone has trauma," I said, and the words felt heavy in the air, weighted with all my unspoken truths they'd never know.

It's the smile, I think. The same one I wear just before diving headfirst into hard things, into the impossible moments that will haunt me long after they've passed. If scars are the proof of injury, then my smile is my scar—a badge I wear to tell the world, "I'm fine," when every piece of me knows otherwise.

The memories come rushing back—fragments of a past that still lingers in the shadows. I was nine years old, clinging to the last bit of innocence I had left. Whatever small piece could remain after a father decides he has more important things than being a father, or when a mother, trying to build a better life, leaves you behind for two years with people who only knew how to harm. So, that sliver of innocence meant everything to me, a fragile remnant of a child who'd seen too much. But even that tiny piece wasn't safe. One summer day, in the most unremarkable way, it was taken, like everything else.

I went to the bathroom—just a simple, everyday act—expecting nothing more than a moment of privacy. I entered as a nine-year-old, and within moments, I was a little girl fighting for her life. Two teenage boys, my cousins—people who should have been my protectors—decided that day to change everything.

I remember it all like it was yesterday. I could hear them at the door, their voices creeping into my space. My small, nervous voice called out, "Go away, I'm using the bathroom." But they didn't leave. My fear mounted, twisting in my stomach as I realized they weren't playing. This was real, and I was in danger. "Stop playin' y'all. I'm trying to use the bathroom," I tried again, my voice shaky.

But the words weren't working. I jumped from the toilet, scanning the tiny room, desperately looking for an escape. There were none—no window in that interior bathroom, no way out. I was trapped. All I could do was brace myself for what was about to be a fight for survival. The door finally swung open, and the struggle began.

They were two teenage boys against a nine-year-old girl; it wasn't a fight, not really. They grabbed me with hands far too strong for a little girl to resist, lifting me as I kicked and screamed, carrying me down the narrow hallway. One held my hands, the other my legs, and I felt every rough drop as I struggled, my body slipping from their grasp only to be yanked back up. Despite being dropped on my back several times, I didn't stop fighting. I screamed for help, even though no one was there to hear. My voice was swallowed up by their laughter, mocking and dismissive, as they carried me toward a darkness I couldn't escape. I twisted and clawed, but I was only nine. I was no match for them.

When it was over, I felt lost, bruised, and broken, carrying a weight no child should ever bear. I turned to an older cousin, hoping he might offer comfort or at least stand as a shield between me and my abusers. But there was no handbook for him—no guide on what to say when your little cousin tells you she was raped.

He raised his hand for a high five, giving me an awkward smile. "I'm glad you fought," he said. "Sounds like you put up a good fight. You should be happy—you're tough." I didn't want to be tough. I wanted to be nine. But I smiled anyway. I showed him my scar, and in that moment, it made him feel better about his response. That was when I learned that people didn't need me to be okay; they just needed me not to make them feel uncomfortable about my pain.

I turned to my mother, desperate for solace, and she did everything a mother could possibly do to try and make it right. But who teaches a mother how to respond when her only child tells her that she was raped? There's no handbook, no guide to help a parent navigate the depths of this kind of pain. She offered me love, she was angry, and she did her best with the tools she had. I could see the confusion in her eyes, the helplessness. She didn't know what else to do, and I didn't want to add to her burden. So, I smiled, I showed her my scar, knowing that my scar had a way of comforting others—even if it couldn't heal me.

The therapist my mother sent me to asked, "Do you want to tell me what happened?" I stared at her, this stranger who believed she had the right to dig into my private hell. I showed her my scar and replied, "No, thank you. It's none of your business." And again, I smiled. Showing people my scar made my "No" a little softer, easier to swallow.

I learned early that people preferred the scar because my smile was easier to handle than my truth. But this smile wasn't a mask; it was there for everyone to see, as real as the pain it covered. My scar was on full display, yet people found it acceptable, even comforting. It made them feel at ease. They looked at my face and saw the smile—a scar so visible, but so easy to overlook. Because no one wanted to confront the darkness behind it.

Even today people may ask "are we seeing your smile or your scar?" That's like asking someone who walks with a limp, "Are you limping or walking?" The answer is yes. So, am I smiling, or am I showing you, my scar? The answer is Yes!

That scar has saved me more times than I can count. I was thirteen the first time a grown man leered at me, his gaze lingering far too long, his words dripping with a thinly veiled inappropriate hunger. He told me I was "beautiful," insisted I should "smile for him." I knew what he wanted. I knew the danger that lurked in his eyes. And yet, when he pushed, I didn't let him see the fear; I showed him my scar. I smiled. That smile gave me a moment to think, to calculate an escape, to save myself from becoming a pedophiles next victim.

The scar stayed, a constant companion. Life continued, relentless, unmoved by my pain. Trauma came in waves, each one hitting before I had a chance to heal from the last. But through it all, I kept smiling, kept showing the world my scar, as if to say, "Look, here I am. I survived." And the scar became a well-used tool in my survival belt.

Today, people look at me—the CEO, the TEDx speaker, the international consultant—and say, "You don't look like what you've been through." I flash my scar, the same practiced smile I've always worn, and think to myself, "I look exactly like what I've been through. You just like the way I wear my scar."

And yet, despite it all, I stand here—unbreakable. I've learned that my smile isn't just my scar; it's a testament. It's the bridge between who I was and who I am, between trauma and triumph. It's the reason I've walked into boardrooms and onto stages, sharing not just the victories but the scars that paved the way. Because the truth is, the scar is a part of me—it's as much a sign of healing as it is of pain.

So, yes, I've endured. But more than that, I've transformed. The same hands that dragged me down could not keep me down, the trauma as driven me to build a life that defies my past. I am here, not in spite of my trauma but because of it. I am smiling, showing you my scar, and living proof that resilience can be born from the darkest of places.

Beyond Survival: Thriving After a Brain Tumor by D. Smith

I remember it just like it was yesterday. It was December of 2010 and a time of year when almost everyone who worked in higher education, looked forward to the end of a grueling fall semester.

As always, I traveled to Ohio to visit my family for the Christmas and New Year holidays. I've often heard people say, "Life is good!" Well, it *was* good! I was working in a career that I absolutely, loved. I was financially secure, and I was in a relationship that was as smooth as my bald head. When in Ohio, I was always surrounded by an amazing close-knit family who loved me to pieces. I always received consistent positive and affirming energy that allowed me to refuel from working so hard throughout the semester. I always say and have always said, life was good --- until it wasn't.

"What's that big bump on the front of your head?" asked my sister.

"I'm not sure," I responded.

"Does it hurt?", she inquired.

"Nah. It doesn't hurt", I said.

"Oh," she said. "Well, you need to go to your doctor and have that checked when you go back to Georgia."

"Okay," I said, nonchalantly. However, in the back of my mind, I was really scared. I went on to enjoy the holidays and festivities with the family as if nothing had ever happened and the brief conversation regarding the bump had not taken place.

In January, when I returned to my home in Georgia, I *did not* make an appointment to see my doctor as instructed. Life got in the way so many times that I, literally, forgot to make the appointment. That was very strange considering I looked at myself every day and the bump was still there, but I chose not to "see" it. This went on for about 2 months until I finally made the appointment in mid-March 2011.

When I saw my primary care physician, he immediately sent me to have a CAT scan. The images from the CAT scan showed nothing. He then, ordered an MRI which was scheduled 1-week after the office visit. Several days later, I found myself lying in a huge MRI imaging machine that was very loud, and it made various weird sounds. Initially, it was very intimidating because I did not know what to expect. I finally settled in and "relaxed" enough to get through the process. The technician provided me with headphones so that I could listen to music. I listened to Anita Baker. It was just me, Anita chillin', and God in the tunnel (which is what I called the machine).

Let's move forward to my next appointment in early April 2011. This appointment was with a brain surgeon. Yes. A brain surgeon! Oh Lord. Here we go. Long story short, it was revealed that I had a benign meningioma tumor on the frontal lobe of my brain. I was informed they grew very slow and that's what caused the bump on the top of my forehead. The surgeon informed me the tumor was about the size of a walnut. Then, he recommended I have a craniotomy to remove it. A what? I'd never heard the word before but quickly got familiar with what was about to happen. Sigh. In short, the surgeon opened my skull, removed the tumor, and put my skull back on. Of course, that's a very simplistic description because it's an extremely complex surgery but you get the picture. I was advised in the initial consultation that the research showed IF a meningioma was to return, it would do so, on average, in 6-years or less. As fate would have it, another benign tumor was discovered in the same area of my brain *in the 6th year* --- which resulted in me having to have *another* craniotomy in January 2017!

Now, mind you, prior to the 1st surgery, I had taken care of the following: 1. Have a will and Living Will prepared 2. Complete medical directives in the event there were complications up to and including death and 3. Make sure all my personal business was in order. That was nerve-racking and that's when having to have the surgery became real!

The Surgery

As I previously mentioned, the 1st craniotomy was in April 2011. Six years later (January 2017), 3 small tumors were discovered in an annual MRI. They were small enough that I had to have several rounds of radiation treatments to stunt their growth. Fortunately, the radiation treatments worked because there was no increase in their size. Thank you, God!

Finding Gratitude in the Journey

Today, I am thriving in spite the past traumas. How? It's very simple. I always focus on the blessings The Creator has given me and there are *so many* things for which I am eternally grateful. My energy is and has always been NOT on what happened to me *but what could have happened in the journey*. Every time I think of God's goodness towards me, I cannot do anything but be thankful! Here's why my heart overflows with gratitude:

1. The tumors were benign. Meaning non-cancerous versus malignant (cancerous). That's a huge blessing that I don't take lightly, nor do I take for granted. I'm so filled with gratitude even as I write this! Thank you, Father!

2. Both craniotomies were super successful. I've had my skull taken off and put back on TWICE and thank God, I had no complications, nor did I need any type of therapy. One day after each of the surgeries, I was very proud that I figured out a simple "word" math problem and I'm not even good at math!

3. Family Support. I have two sisters who came to stay with me for a whole month to help nurse me back to health by giving me my medicines, making sure I ate well, taking me to doctors' appointments etc.

4. *Complete healing*, however, took about 1-year but I was in it to win it!

My thoughts were not on what was happening and questioning, "Why me?" My thoughts were always focused on gratitude. There are so many ways the situation could have turned out! If anyone is faced with anything traumatic that life throws your way, please consider incorporating prayer and/or meditation into your daily routine. Always give gratitude for "what is" knowing "what is" could be worse.

From Pain to Purpose by Wytishia Bly

My trauma started at a very young age, although I am a country girl from Milledgeville, Georgia. I grew up in Boston, Massachusetts. Being a country girl, I was used to moving slower, however, growing up in Boston, everything was fast. At the young age of 12 years old, I experienced rape by a guy in my neighborhood and his friends.

We lived in the projects in Boston. The neighborhood was very rough. I knew the guy that raped me. We went to school together. This was one of a few events that led to my trauma.

The second was having an abortion at a very young age. I had an abortion at the age of 15. My mom did not think it would be wise for me to keep a baby at that age. I had to be put to sleep because I couldn't stay up for something like that. At the age of 18, I was held at gunpoint for 5 1/2 hours. I was held hostage by my boyfriend at the time. He came to my grandmother's house to kill me. Thankfully, it just ended with him going to jail, and I'm alive today. I know trauma better than anybody.

I believe because my grandmother raised me in the church that that is where my strength came from. I know how to pray, and each time I went through these things, I prayed. I feel like having a strong relationship with God will see you through anything. I'm a forgiven person, so I didn't let it weigh me down.

Being held hostage at a young age, at any age, is so scary. I truly thought I was going to die that day, but again, God served just to allow it. I'm thankful for my village. My family has stuck by me through it all.

Today, I have been in therapy for eight years. Therapy has helped me forgive, move on, and start over fresh. I'm so grateful to my therapist. She has become a real friend to me. We take time each session to reflect on where I am today. The goal is not to hold onto your past. You might as well stay in it if you're gonna do that. I let go of my past, and the moment I did, I began to heal. Now I'm the author of a book that tells my full story. It's called "From a Pawn to a Queen." Writing my book was also therapeutic for me, and I love the fact that it touches other young women. I am now connected to an organization called Women on the Rise. This organization supports women who have been incarcerated and are justice-impacted. I feel amazing being part of something so special.

I want to tell others who have experienced trauma: Don't sit in it, don't stay in it, and don't blame yourself. I am a living witness that there is light at the end of the tunnel.

Moment of Stillness by Maxine Williams Wright

When I was younger, I never had problems with employment. Salaries were substantial enough to support the needs and wants of myself and my sons after my divorce. I managed to live in nice communities and surrounded them with meaningful and effective perceptions. Financial hardship struck me during my middle-aged years. Somehow when I reached my mid 50s employers were not quick to offer employment opportunities. I knew my age was a factor, but employers will never tell you the primary reason for no consideration was age discrimination. Why should they hire someone in their mid-50s when there were so many younger applicants?

I started substitute teaching to have a source of income and to keep my mind occupied. Plus, I worked 15 hours a week at a college but didn't receive consistent compensation due to their financial instability. I subbed for several months at different schools and the longest assignment was at Marietta High School. I used my savings and credit cards to keep the household functioning. After I depleted my savings and maxed out my credit cards, I humbled myself before my family and friends. I had always been the giver and not the borrower. I didn't understand why I was going through such hardship.

For the first time in my life, I had to ask for help. It took everything in me to ask my family and my ministry members for financial support. I recalled donating on many occasions to others in the ministry and to family members, but now I was humbled to the point of asking for financial support. I thought about giving up and walking away from everything and everybody. I wanted to get in my car and drive until I utilized my remaining resources. In other words, I wanted to disappear and just exist somewhere else. The only person I didn't want to hurt and to worry was my mother. She was the reason I didn't submit to the outlandish impulses. Those I had supported and assisted were not there for me, but I managed to press on and thanked God for the hearts He touched who came to my rescue. I will forever be grateful.

The Most High sent many angels to care for me. Friends who knew I wasn't working mailed checks to me and some placed cash in my hands when I saw them at church. One evening I was on my way home and saw a family on the side of the road holding a sign. It truly touched my heart because it was a woman and man with their baby. The woman was holding the sign, and the man was holding the baby. The sign read "Please help, trying to get home, we need gas and food." I stopped my car and gave them $5.00. When I got home later that evening a check for $500.00 was in my mailbox made payable to me. I knew The Most High God was still using His chosen people to bless me. By sharing what I had God multiplied my act of kindness by one hundred.

During my time of working part-time and being unemployed I discovered many talents God had given me. I wrote my first stage play, created a collection of wall art, vases, and candleholders, and became an interior designer. I used those gifts from God as a source of income. It took stillness and unemployment to get my attention. Sometimes it takes an emphatic change in your life to direct you to your divine path.

The Pastor of my church knew I was experiencing financial hardship. He asked another church member who was in a position to assist me with employment. I was so grateful that my Pastor cared enough to think about my wellbeing. I was hired as a contractor and the assignment had potential to turn into a full-time position, so I had confidence everything was going to be alright.

It felt good working nine to five again. I shared an office with another member from church that the Pastor also recommended. We became good friends and helped each other through our struggles. Some days were hard for me, and she knew exactly what to say. Some days were hard for her and God guided my words just for her. Then after a few months on the assignments we were told that our assignments were over. I went into a state of panic, but I managed to calm myself as I spoke with my coworker. When the time came, I said my goodbyes and was back to thinking about other options. During the drive home I had time to think. I decided to focus on my creativity since that was a gift, while I sought out employment opportunities. Having that mindset encouraged me to continue the journey.

The first morning of being home without having to go to work, I went into my home office which was my favorite room. I sat there in silence and from the pit of my stomach a piercing squeal filled the room. I ended up on my knees in my bedroom beside my bed. I prayed like I had never prayed before. I screamed over and over to God, "I can't go back, I can't go back!" I couldn't go back to having nothing and feeling hopeless. I stayed there until I was exhausted. After pleading out to God, I managed to compose myself and returned to my office. I sat behind my desk dazed and motionless for a couple of hours. There was nothing else I could do. It was in God's hands.

While in my moment of stillness, I received a phone call from an unrecognized number. The woman asked, "May I speak to Ms. Wright?" I answered, "This is she." My mood was still somewhat subdued. I sat there waiting but didn't know what I was waiting for. My mind was empty, my spirit was drained, and yet my heart was beating. The woman began to talk about a position I had applied for, but I had no idea about the position since I had applied for numerous positions. She asked if I still had an interest, so I excitedly told her, "Yes," without knowing the position she spoke about because it had been too long ago. She then stated, "I have to fill this position today, I've called two other applicants, but they didn't answer, you're my third call. Do you want the position?" That's what I was waiting for the call. He arranged for the two previous calls not to be answered, so I could answer the third call.

At that point I thought someone was playing on the phone, but I still accepted her offer. She hired me over the phone without an interview. She heard the excitement in my voice, and I praised God while she was on the phone. I kept saying thank You God, I couldn't restrain myself. She calmly said, "Yes, it's okay to thank Him." She told me to report the next week to complete the new hire documents. I accepted the offer without knowing the details of the position since I didn't want her to know I didn't remember. After the call I researched and located the position which I had saved on my computer. I reported on the required date and time without knowing all the details of the position because it didn't matter since I knew it was a gift from The Most High God.

Even though I worked as a contractor prior to accepting the offer, I still didn't have enough to pay my mortgage during the timeframe. My income had been reduced by 70% and I was only able to pay the utilities, car notes, and other essentials. After I accepted the fulltime permanent position, I strategically planned to set funds aside to present to the mortgage company. I knew the mortgage company would require a lump sum for the arrears. The plan was in motion, but I just needed a little more time. Every evening, I entered the subdivision not knowing what I would find. I ignored the foreclosure notice and the phone calls from the mortgage company. I just couldn't handle anymore stress. When I turned on my street, I prayed not to see my belongings on the curbside. Thank You God was all I could say each day I came home from work. The house had three levels with five bedrooms, four bathrooms and a finished basement. It was indeed a haven for many souls along the way. My door was opened for family and friends who needed to stay a night and those who needed a place to live. At the time I didn't realize the similarities I had with my mother. I was indeed my mother's daughter. Mom fed and sheltered many throughout her life in her home. She was a jewel when it came to sharing and helping others.

The consequences of not paying my mortgage for a year marinated throughout my entire body. The night before I planned to make the call was indeed a restless night. While at work the next day I took a break and went to a secluded area. I took deep breaths as I called the mortgage company. The customer service representative needed my personal information. When she retrieved my file, I told her I was ready to make payment arrangements. I asked about the foreclosure, the allotted timeframe to get caught up, and the amount I had to pay. She stated, "Your home is not under foreclosure." At that point I was confused. Then I mentioned the notice I had received in the mail months ago. The representative said, "Your home was on the list, then your home was removed from the list."

I didn't quite understand, my head started to spin, and I leaned against a wall and said, "Thank You God!" I got myself together and asked about the amount I needed to pay to get caught up. Representative responded, "Just your scheduled mortgage payment and I will put the debt owed on the backend." My eyes filled with praise, my heart leaped with joyfulness, and my mind absorbed His greatness! Right at that moment I knew The Most High God removed my name from the list of foreclosures. Once again God had interceded on my behalf. His miraculous plan!

The Most High God heard my voice, saw my dire need, and felt my pain. He orchestrated the entire situation. His process tuned my character, fashioned my perspectives, extended my endurance, and instilled me with strength. He knows what call you should answer and what list you should not be on. Just make sure your name is on God's list, and you answer His call!

Even though I experienced many adversities, God's hands were always on me. There was more work for me to do for His kingdom. When there's purpose for your life, He will sustain you in order for you to become the person you are destined to be.

When I think about His goodness
It takes me to a time
Was down to my last dime
There were situations I couldn't handle
Wanted to throw in the towel, yell surrender
Yet, He reminded me of all the countless possibilities meant
to be
All unforeseen talents waiting to be released.

—Plays—

Down Center
The Corner
Hats
The Manifest

—Books—

Testimonies, God's Unfolding Miracles (Inspirational)
FirstBorn (Fantasy, Romance, Horror, Thriller, Mystery)

Unbreakable: A Survivor's Testimony

Pieces of Me (Poetry)
Toby and Sheba (Children's Literature)

—Music—
Actuality (Spoken Word)
Georgia Woman, Mississippi Man (Blues Collaboration)

Maxine Williams Wright
MaxWill Productions, LLC
www.maxwillproductions.com

Faith Over Fear by TeaDrama

Several years ago, I was presented with an extraordinary opportunity—a chance to step away from the comfort and stability of the organization where I had worked faithfully for over 15 years. It wasn't an easy decision, but the offer was compelling. In short, I was offered a voluntary severance package, one that included an extension of my current salary for 17 months along with benefits.

The option tickled my ear because I had a deep-down desire to work as a contractor.
I listened distinctly for the voice of God before I made the decision to move forward with exiting the company. After the last hoorays, I allowed myself one week of rest to clear my mind and prepare for the next chapter of my journey.

Determined to make the most of this transition, I then proceeded to attend company paid career counseling sessions. The classes allowed me to assess personal skills, values, aspirations, and to tap into my network of resources. They also provided me with tools to tailor my resume and cover letter to any journey I was willing to pursue.

On days without classes, I was either attending job fairs or tirelessly seeking and applying for positions.

Weeks passed, and while I interviewed for several roles, none of them felt like the right fit. Despite the lack of immediate success, I never lost hope or doubted my decision. I was determined in my heart, and no doubt was in my mind, that I had moved according to God's plan and not my own.

Three months after leaving the company, I successfully negotiated a contract position at a favorable salary, complete with a travel per-diem. Over the next eight months, I further negotiated a partially remote working arrangement, found steady and affordable temporary housing within walking distance of the job site, and gained the trust of my client. They entrusted me to handle both familiar and unfamiliar systems, and I approached each challenge without fear.

It was a season of faith over fear.

The job brought its share of challenges. In those "mountain moments," I learned to lean fully on God, the master of my soul. Along the way, I acquired new software skills and added them to my career toolkit.

Being away from home meant my husband often lived the bachelor life. To bridge the gap, I brought him to visit several times. Although the mountain travel was trying—with me battling personal summers (aka hot flashes) and him bundling up against the chill—we cherished those treasured moments together.

During this season of working and collecting a severance salary, I was blessed to provide assistance to friends and family members in ways I never could have imagined. Initially, I had planned to save the surplus for personal use, but God had a greater purpose. My mission became one of servitude and sacrifice rather than personal satisfaction.

Looking back, I see how this journey was orchestrated by God, teaching me to trust Him fully, lean into His guidance, and embrace the opportunities He placed before me. Every step, every decision, and every challenge had a purpose. This chapter in my life wasn't just about career growth; it was about growing in faith, serving others, and finding fulfillment in obedience to His will.

A Journey from Darkness to Light by ANONYMOUS 3

Twelve years ago, a single moment of terror forever altered the course of my life. I was working a quiet evening shift at Dots, a retail store, when the sound of the door chime broke the stillness. I glanced up, expecting a customer—but instead, a man stepped in, wearing a hood and a bandana across his face. In his hand, a gun gleamed ominously.

"You know what it is," he said, his voice cold and commanding.

I froze. My body felt like it was made of stone, but my mind raced, overwhelmed by fear. He barked at me to open the register, and I fumbled desperately with the buttons, my shaking hands refusing to cooperate. The cold, heavy barrel of the gun pressed against the back of my neck, sending waves of panic through me. It felt like an eternity before I finally managed to open the drawer. He swept the money into a bag as my coworker opened the safe. And just as suddenly as he arrived, he was gone, leaving behind silence, chaos, and a version of me I no longer recognized.

As the adrenaline faded, I found myself sick to my stomach. The shock turned into anger as I watched the police arrive, their lack of urgency adding insult to injury. To them, it seemed like just another robbery. To me, it was the moment my sense of safety shattered.

I quit the next day. There was no way I could step foot back in that store. My family rallied around me, promising to help with expenses until I could find another job. But financial support couldn't heal the emotional scars.

I withdrew from the world. Alcohol became my escape, numbing the pain and fear I couldn't face. For months, I barely left the house, avoiding not just Dots but the entire neighborhood. Anything that reminded me of that night—a gunshot on TV, the chime of a store door—was enough to send me spiraling back into the terror of that moment. Nightmares plagued me, and even the smallest errands required a family escort. I felt like a prisoner in my own mind, shackled by fear.

But life has a way of nudging you forward, even when you're convinced you can't take another step. Slowly, almost imperceptibly, I began to rebuild. I found a new job, one that helped me regain a sense of purpose. The nightmares became less frequent. I ventured out on my own, testing the boundaries of my comfort zone.

Today, I stand on the other side of that darkness. I can watch movies and shows with gun violence without feeling the panic rise in my chest. I can walk into a store without scanning for exits or calculating escape routes. Most importantly, I've regained my independence, no longer needing someone to accompany me every time I leave the house.

In a surprising twist, I even found myself maintaining a rapport with someone who, I later learned, had committed an armed robbery. It was a testament to how far I'd come—that I could separate my trauma from their actions and see them as a person rather than a symbol of my past.

This journey wasn't easy, and it wasn't quick. But it taught me that healing is possible, even when it feels out of reach. The fear that once controlled me no longer defines me. Instead, it serves as a reminder of my strength, my resilience, and the power of choosing to move forward, one step at a time.

A Journey of Survival and Purpose by Dana "MzDanaK" Jones

Life has a way of throwing unexpected challenges our way, and for me, it came crashing down in a series of unimaginable events. At just 17 years old, I experienced not one but three strokes within a single month. I was preparing for a date in the bathroom when I suddenly felt unwell and had to be rushed to the hospital. Little did I know, I was fighting for my life on that drive.

My mother later told me that as I lay in a coma for a month, she spoke to my father over the phone, explaining what the nurse had told her—that I had suffered three strokes, possibly even a fourth. I'll never forget the weight of that truth. Those strokes changed my life forever, but they didn't defeat me.

I'm not saying that birth control was the cause, but I started experiencing persistent headaches after I began taking it, and not long after, the strokes followed. I often wonder about the connection, but regardless of the cause, what truly matters is how I found the strength to survive.

My children became my reason to fight. I had my oldest daughter before the strokes, and even while in a coma, I remember pleading with God, "What about my daughter?" She gave me a reason to pull through, a reason to hold on. Then, after my recovery, I had my youngest daughter. She became my second miracle—a reason to keep living, to strive for a better version of myself every day.

I'm not just surviving—I'm thriving. Today, I am an actress with a disability, a spoken word artist, and an emerging author. My autobiography, *In the Blink of an Eye*, shares my journey of survival, resilience, and rediscovering purpose. Through my story, I want to inspire others to live life fully, not just exist in it.

I model from time to time, pour my soul into spoken word, and embrace every opportunity to learn and grow. My strokes might have slowed me down physically, but they lit a fire in my spirit. I see myself doing so much more in the near future. I want the world to know this: *I am a brainstem stroke survivor. I am a fighter. I am living proof that even in the face of life-altering challenges, there is hope, purpose, and light.*

This is MzDana's World—a world of strength, creativity, and boundless determination. I hope my story inspires others to find their own reason to live, to fight, and to truly embrace the gift of life.

About T. S. Edwards aka MiZZ Entertainment

A Symphony of Talent, Service, and Entertainment

T. S. Edwards or Teresa, affectionately known as "MiZZ Entertainment," is a dynamic force in the entertainment industry, weaving a tapestry of diverse experiences and talents. With an MBA from Kennesaw State University and over two decades of distinguished service in the U.S. Air Force, Edwards has seamlessly transitioned from global military operations to commanding stages and boardrooms alike.

As an entrepreneur, author, executive producer, playwright, and music consultant, Edwards brings unparalleled energy and expertise to every endeavor. Her magnetic presence as a speaker and host has electrified audiences across hundreds of events, collaborating with industry titans such as

Warner Bros. Discovery, AT&T, and the Technology Association of Georgia.

Edwards' journey from telecommunications professional to entertainment mogul is a testament to her adaptability and passion. As co-founder of Terror Dome Entertainment, LLC, she channels her creative vision into groundbreaking video and music productions. Her commitment to social causes shines through Silence the Tears, a non-profit she founded to support abused children. And From School to Possibilities, a non-profit she found to support minority high school students interested in media and entertainment.

Featured in CanvasRebel and VoyageATL, Edwards' influence extends beyond the spotlight. She dedicates her time as a KSU Executive MBA Program coach and serves on numerous entertainment and technology boards, shaping the future of the industry.

Her artistic repertoire is as diverse as her skill set, spanning television shows, podcasts, plays, movie shorts, and books. The "Adventures of Hildie and Carlos" children's book series stands as a heartwarming tribute to her role as a grandmother.

In every role—be it entrepreneur, veteran, consultant, mentor, or family woman—T. S. Edwards brings an infectious enthusiasm and unwavering dedication. Those who work with her don't just become clients; they become part of a legacy built on passion, creativity, and the relentless pursuit of excellence.

T. S. Edwards doesn't just entertain; she inspires, innovates, and ignites the potential in others, truly embodying the essence of "MiZZ Entertainment" in every aspect of her multifaceted career.

Connect With T. S. Edwards

IG: unbreakable_ast

FB: unbreakable – A Survivor's Testimony

Email: info@terrordomeent.com

Check Out These Websites

www.TSEdwardsAuthor.com

www.TerrorDomeEntertainment.com

www.HildieAndCarlos.com

www.FromSchoolToPossibilities.org

www.FathersUnitedForJustice.org

TEDWARDS
Creative Guru

TERROR DOME
ENTERTAINMENT

SEDWARDS

Creative Guru

www.TSEdwardsAuthor.com

Be Kind To Each Other!

Love One Another!

Keep God First!

T. S. Edwards